Under the Microscope

In **Rivers, Lakes, and Ponds**

Sabrina Crewe

Consultant:
Professor Anne K. Camper,
Montana State University

CHELSEA
CLUBHOUSE
An Imprint of Chelsea House Publishers

Chelsea Clubhouse
An imprint of Chelsea House
132 West 31st Street
New York NY 10001

Library of Congress Cataloging-in-Publication Data

Crewe, Sabrina.
  In rivers, lakes, and ponds / Sabrina Crewe ; consultant, Professor Anne K. Camper.
     p. cm. -- (Under the microscope)
  Includes index.
  ISBN 978-1-60413-826-9
  1. Freshwater microbiology--Juvenile literature. 2. Microscopy--Juvenile literature. I. Title. II. Series.

  QR105.5.C74 2010
  502.8'2--dc22

                           2009050499

Chelsea Clubhouse books are available at special discounts when purchased in bulk quantities for businesses, associations, institutions, or sales promotions. Please call our Special Sales Department in New York at (212) 967-8800 or (800) 322-8755.

You can find Chelsea Clubhouse on the World Wide Web at http://www.chelseahouse.com

Text design by Sabine Beaupré
Illustrations by Stefan Chabluk
Originated by Discovery Books
Composition by Discovery Books
Cover printed by Bang Printing, Brainerd, MN
Book printed and bound by Bang Printing, Brainerd, MN
Date printed: May 2010
Printed in the United States of America

10 9 8 7 6 5 4 3 2 1

Acknowledgments
We would like to thank the following for permission to reproduce photographs: Dennis Kunkel Microscopy, Inc.: pp. 15, 17, 21 top; National Park Service: p. 26; Science Photo Library: pp. 5 (Stefanie Reichelt), 6 (Eric Grave), 8 (M. I. Walker), 9 (Eye of Science), 10 (Power and Syred), 11 (Gerd Guenther), 13 bottom (M. I. Walker), 14 (Jan Hinsch), 16 (Kent Wood), 18 (Sinclair Stammers), 19 (John Walsh), 20 (M. I. Walker), 22 (Martin Dohrn), 23 (Gary Meszaros), 24 (David M. Phillips), 25 top (Michael Abbey), 27 bottom (Eye of Science); Shutterstock Images: pp. 4 (Yurchyks), 13 top (Christopher Meade), 21 bottom (Jubal Harshaw), 25 bottom (Hagit Berkovich), 27 top (Marco Regalia), 29 top (Devon Sarian), 29 bottom (Anthony Harris); US Department of Agriculture: p. 12.

Contents

Some words are **bold** the first time they appear in the text. These words are explained in the glossary at the back of this book.

Watery World

We may live on land, but there is water all around us. Somewhere near your home, there is a pond or a stream, a river or a lake.

Microscopic life

Wherever there is water, there is a tiny world of living things, or **organisms**. Organisms too small for us to see are called **microorganisms**. If they were your size, you would think they were alien beings from another planet. But some are so small that thousands of them can fit into a drop of water!

Many different kinds of microorganisms live in water. They can be animals, plants, or something in between. To visit this miniature watery world, we need a microscope. The microscope will reveal creatures that you never knew existed.

Above and below

We're going to look in ponds and lakes, where the water is still and microorganisms live on or near the surface. We are also going to see creatures that live at the bottom of rivers and streams, clinging to rocks or plants as the water rushes over them.

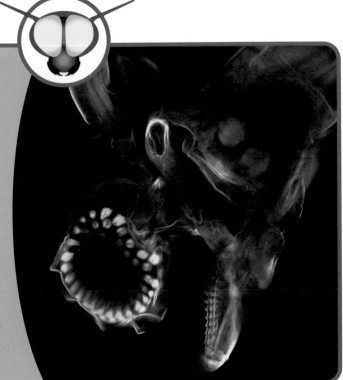

Micro-Monster

This is the head of a *Polyphemus* water flea. The *Polyphemus* has one giant eye (bottom left) that it uses to find its **prey**. In real life, the whole flea is only about 1 millimeter across, or about the length of this line - .

Actinopods are a type of protozoa. They are also sometimes called "sun animalcules" because their axopods, or thin limbs, look like rays of the Sun. Actinopods use these axopods to catch their prey.

Protists

Many water-dwelling microorganisms belong to a group of organisms called **protists**. Protists aren't plants or animals. Some—known as **protozoa**—behave like animals. Others—often called **algae**—are more like plants. Most protists, whether they are protozoa or algae, have only one **cell**. But even with just one cell, they can make or capture food, move around, and reproduce.

Protozoa

Some protozoa are flagellates, which means they have long strands on their bodies that they beat back and forth to move around. Others are ciliates—they have cilia, or hairs, to propel them along. Amoebas are slow-moving blobs of protozoa, but they can capture and eat other creatures living in the water, including **microanimals**.

Plant-like protists

Algae, or plant-like protists, are similar to plants because they make their own food through the process of **photosynthesis**. As you will see, many of them don't resemble plants that grow on land. Diatoms, for example, look like shiny disks or sticks.

We're going to take a look at several types of protists that you might find under a microscope in rivers, lakes, and ponds.

Domains of Life

Biologists often divide living things on Earth into three **domains**, which are shown below. Eukaryota are living things with a certain kind of cell called a **eukaryotic** cell. These cells are quite complex and ordered, with a **nucleus** and other separate parts. Protists, plants, animals, and **fungi** are all part of the eukaryotic domain. The other domains are those of **bacteria** and **archaea**. (We'll be looking at them later.) These organisms have simpler cells called **prokaryotic** cells.

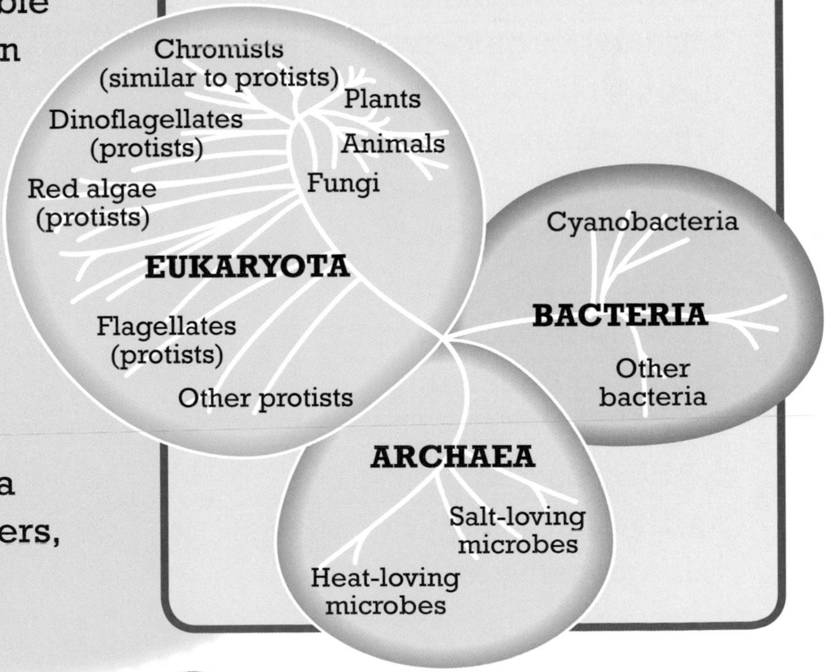

Chromists
(similar to protists)

Dinoflagellates
(protists)

Plants

Animals

Red algae
(protists)

Fungi

EUKARYOTA

Flagellates
(protists)

Other protists

Cyanobacteria

BACTERIA

Other
bacteria

ARCHAEA

Salt-loving
microbes

Heat-loving
microbes

Ciliates

Ciliates are protozoa, or animal-like protists. There are thousands of different types of ciliates. What they have in common are the tiny hairs called cilia that grow from their bodies. They use their cilia like oars in the water to move around and to stop.

Many ciliates are shaped like fish, which makes them a good shape for moving quickly through the water. Other ciliates live attached to an object, such as a river plant or a rock. Whether they are free to swim around or stuck in one place, ciliates feed by catching and eating other microorganisms.

Some ciliates, called peritrichs, have cilia that form fringes around their mouths. The cilia create currents that bring food particles toward them. Peritrichs usually live in colonies, or groups, attached to a surface by long stalks.

Swimming around

The *Paramecium* is a ciliate that swims near the surface of ponds, lakes, and rivers. It shoots out sharp-tipped threads, like darts, to attach itself to a surface while it eats its prey. It also has poisonous darts to fire at other creatures that try to prey on it!

Staying put

Suctoria are a type of ciliate that live attached by a stalk to algae or other things. They reach out for prey with their **tentacles**, which have sticky pads on the ends. When they catch something to eat, suctoria suck out their prey's insides!

Micro-Scientist

Scientists who study animals are called zoologists. Protozoologists study everything to do with protozoa. They may focus on protozoa that get into drinking water and make people sick.

Micro-Monster

Some ciliates, such as the *Didinium* (below left), can swallow prey bigger than themselves. The *Didinium* is engulfing a *Paramecium* (right).

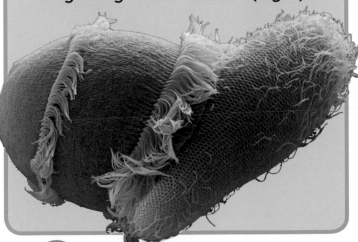

The amoeba on the left is extending its false feet to capture another amoeba. These amoebas have been magnified 230 times.

Amoebas

The body of an amoeba is a little like a blob of jelly. But don't be deceived: these slow-moving protozoa can catch prey just as well as any animal.

How Small Is Small?

The biggest species of amoeba are up to 5 millimeters across, so you could see them without a microscope. The smallest are smaller than 10 **micrometers**, and there are 1,000 micrometers in a millimeter.

Stalking prey

Amoebas live and hunt for food at the bottom of lakes and ponds. They have little branches on their bodies, called false feet, which they extend to explore with.

If the false foot finds something to eat, the amoeba flows around the prey until it has engulfed it. The amoeba then dissolves the food, absorbing the **nutrients** it needs.

Dividing, doubling, and drying out

Amoebas are made of just one large cell. When they are ready to reproduce, they divide their cell. The nucleus at the center of the cell splits into two. Then the amoeba stretches and divides, soon separating to form two identical amoebas, each with its own nucleus.

Amoebas can only function in water. But if the pond they live in dries up, they do not die. Instead they go into an inactive state called a cyst. When the water returns, amoebas come back to life.

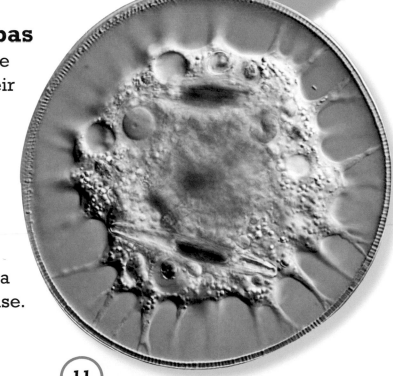

This amoeba lives in ponds and has a thin shell. It holds onto the inside of its shell with several false feet.

Shelled amoebas

A few amoebas have hard shells over their soft bodies. These shells are called tests, and they are made of particles of sand or other matter found in the water. The test protects the amoeba and acts as a disguise.

Algae

You will have seen algae, or plant-like protists, even though most of them are microscopic. This is because many of them mass together to form chains and clumps on the water's surface that we can see clearly.

Some algae, such as *Spirogyra*, form long chains of single cells. Others, such as *Chlorella*, are single cells shaped like balls. These algae clump together to form a mass.

Why are algae green?

Algal cells are green because they contain a substance called chlorophyll. They use chlorophyll during photosynthesis. Some algae contain other colors, too, such as brown, yellow, and red.

These fishponds are different colors because they have various kinds of algae growing on their surfaces.

Volvox is an interesting alga found in shallow water. The colony forms a ball of a clear jelly substance. The small balls inside the big ball are "daughter" cells forming their own colonies.

How Small Is Small?

A *Volvox* colony could be up to 1 millimeter across. Inside, there may be 50,000 *Volvox*!

Conjugation

Most algae reproduce by dividing themselves. But some have another way of reproducing, called conjugation. Conjugation happens when one alga passes the insides of its cell to another. *Spirogyra*, shown here, lines up whole chains of cells to do this. The insides of cells in one chain flow into the opposite cell in the other chain. It leaves one cell empty, as you can see, but the opposite one becomes a new, stronger cell called a spore. Spores can survive without water if a pond dries up or freezes. They come back to life when the water returns.

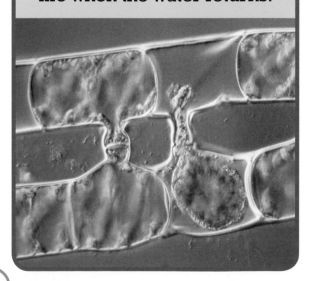

Diatoms

Diatoms do not look like plants, but they are in fact a kind of algae, or plant-like protist. Diatoms are everywhere in water, but they are so small we can't see them unless they form a large clump. Sometimes they do this on the surface of a rock, where they may look like a brown-colored piece of carpet.

Shimmering shapes

An outer shell, or frustule, encases every diatom. Frustules are made of a hard material called silica. Silica is what glass is made of, and it gives diatoms their shimmering appearance.

Diatoms are microscopic algae found in oceans and in freshwater (the water found in rivers and most lakes and ponds).

Although they have only one cell, diatoms come in some wonderful shapes and patterns. They are all symmetrical, which means one side matches the other. Some, called centric diatoms, form a symmetrical circle around a central point. Others, known as pennate diatoms, have symmetrical left and right halves.

Photosynthesis

Diatoms are plant-like because they use photosynthesis to produce their own food. The process requires sunlight, so diatoms live near the surface of water. During photosynthesis, they absorb carbon dioxide from the water and then release oxygen.

Most of the diatoms found in ponds and lakes are pennate diatoms, like this one. They are symmetrical along a central line.

Southern Sr. High Media Center
Harwood, Maryland 20776

Microanimals

When you think of animals, you may think of creatures such as bears and dogs. But insects, worms, and other small creatures are also animals. Some animals are so small that we can only see them with a microscope. Others are a few millimeters long, and we can spot them if we look carefully or use a magnifying glass. Many of these microanimals live in the water.

Cells and eggs

Microanimals can be just as small as protists, but they have many cells. They also have a brain and organs, such as a stomach. And they do not split in half to reproduce. Many lay eggs in which their young develop. Others, like the *Hydra*, produce buds.

Planarians

Tiny worms called planarians are very common in still waters. They live under rocks or plants at the bottom of ponds, away from the light.

When a planarian comes across some prey, it arches its body over its victim and presses it down to the bottom of the pond. Then it eats the prey by sucking at it with a mouth tube.

Planarians appear to have eyes, but the black dots are in fact light detectors that help them avoid light.

Micro-Monster

This *Hydra* is a microanimal that is only a couple of millimeters long in real life. The *Hydra's* mouth (top center) is circled by tentacles. Each tentacle contains a pointed thread that the *Hydra* fires at its prey. As the threads paralyze the prey, the tentacles surround and trap it. Then the *Hydra* swallows it up. On the right you can see that a new *Hydra*, called a bud, is growing out of the parent.

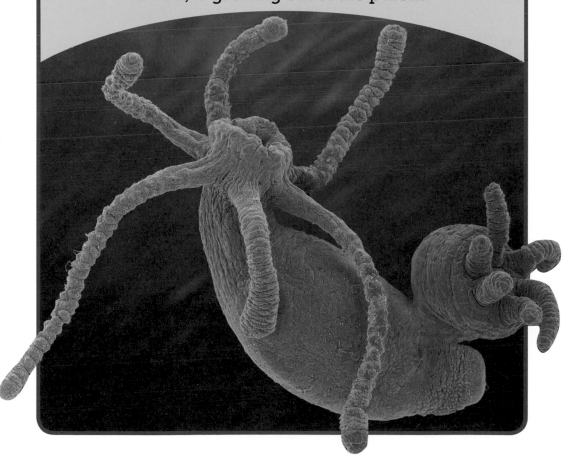

Conochilus rotifers form a ball by joining the bases of their feet together. Their bodies radiate outward from the center. The rotifers beat their cilia in time with each other to spin their colony along through the water.

Rotifers

Rotifers are microanimals that live in lakes, ponds, and all still waters. Some kinds are as small as 200 micrometers across, while others are as big as 1.5 millimeters. That's still a pretty small animal!

Spinning wheels

Under the microscope, there is one sure way to identify a rotifer. It appears to have two spinning wheels on top of its head. The wheels are in fact crowns of cilia that whirl around in the water, creating tiny waves that help pull prey into the rotifer's mouth.

Sticky parts and shells

Rotifers have sticky parts that allow them to attach themselves to other objects. Many live attached to plants or rocks. Others stick together in clumps and move through the water together.

Some rotifers have shells to protect them. Others make their own protection. The *Floscularia* is a rotifer that builds tubes made out of gluey pellets. It forms the pellets in a little scoop and then sticks them on top of each other, one by one, to form a wall. It builds the wall around itself, like a tube made of microscopic bricks.

You can see a *Floscularia* peeking out of the top of its tube. If it is disturbed, it ducks back inside. Attached to the tube are three eggs (top right) and two smaller rotifers.

Rotifer Reproduction

For most of the year, female rotifers lay eggs in the pond that hatch into other females. When the weather begins to get cold, however, some rotifers lay a different type of egg that produces a male. When the male hatches, it mates with a female and then dies. Then the female produces a third type of egg that has been **fertilized** by the male —a tough egg that can survive in the water all winter. In the spring, these eggs hatch into females.

Crustaceans

We've probably all seen pictures of large crustaceans—crabs, lobsters, and giant shrimp. But there are also microscopic versions of these creatures in water near you!

Micro-Monster

The one-eyed cyclops is a copepod. It gets its name from a legendary one-eyed monster because it, too, has only one eye: the black dot near the bottom of this picture. Beneath the cyclops' tail (at the top of the image) are sacs carrying eggs.

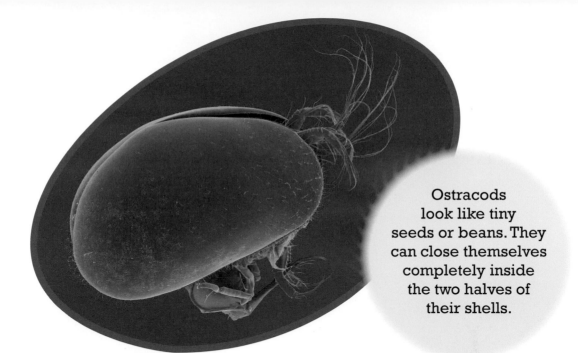

Ostracods look like tiny seeds or beans. They can close themselves completely inside the two halves of their shells.

Outside skeleton

The name *crustacean* is a clue to what these microanimals are like. They are covered by an outer crust, which is really their skeleton. Mini-crustaceans in rivers, lakes, and ponds include three main types: cladocerans (also called water fleas), copepods, and ostracods.

Daphnia

Daphnia are a type of water flea, or cladoceran. The way they move around in water is similar to a flea hopping through the air. *Daphnia* filter tiny organisms out of the water through several pairs of feet. Then they feed on the organisms.

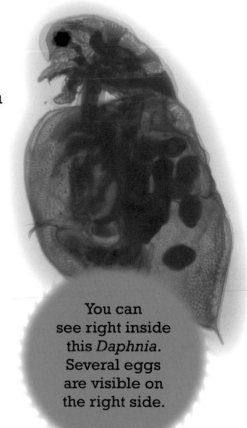

You can see right inside this *Daphnia*. Several eggs are visible on the right side.

These mosquito larvae are hanging below the water's surface. They breathe air through tubes that stick out above the water.

From Water to Air

The microanimals we've looked at so far live their whole lives in the water. Let's take a look at some insects that start their lives as water microorganisms but then move into the air.

Young mosquitoes

Mosquitoes lay their eggs on the water's surface. After a few days, the eggs hatch and out come **larvae**. Larvae are the young of mosquitoes and other insects. A mosquito larva hangs just below the water's surface. The larva will become a pupa, which is a resting stage for an insect as it turns into an adult. After a few days, an adult mosquito emerges above the water. It dries off its body and wings and flies away.

Dragonfly nymphs

Young dragonflies, called nymphs, live in the water, where they grow big enough to be seen without a microscope. They can breathe in water through gills, which are flaps on their bodies like those on a fish. The nymphs live in water until they are ready to become adults. Then they go onto land and become pupae. Soon, an adult emerges.

Micro-Monster

The dragonfly nymph preys on microorganisms and tiny fish in the water. It has a secret weapon for catching prey—its lower lip. It shoots out its lip like a spear, and two hooks at the tip grab hold of its prey.

Bacteria and Cyanobacteria

Bacteria are the smallest and most numerous of organisms. They are everywhere: in you, inside and outside your home, and in water.

Simple cell

Every bacterium is formed from one simple cell. The difference between the bacterium and other life-forms is that its single cell lacks a nucleus. Simple cells without nuclei are called prokaryotic cells. As we saw earlier, prokaryotic organisms have their own domains.

A special kind of bacteria

Most bacteria feed on organic matter, such as plants or animals.

Bacteria come in many shapes and sizes. They reproduce by dividing themselves into two identical cells, and they can multiply very quickly. Several of these bacteria are dividing. They have been magnified about 12,000 times.

Spirulina is a cyanobacteria that forms spiralled chains of cells.

But some bacteria that live in water use photosynthesis to make their own food. This group of bacteria is called **cyanobacteria**. They are similar to algae—in fact, they were known as "blue-green algae" until scientists figured out they were a type of bacteria. Many kinds of cyanobacteria live in mats on top of the water where they can get the most sunlight.

Biofilm

Large communities of algae and bacteria form a film, known as **biofilm**, on surfaces of rivers, lakes, and ponds. Biofilms also form on rocks in water—you may have come into contact with this slippery surface. A biofilm starts with a few bacteria. It soon forms a slime, or film, that other **microbes** become attached to. Biofilms can be harmful or useful. Some contain "bad" bacteria that cause diseases in animals.

But useful bacteria in biofilms can eat up harmful matter in polluted water. In this way, they help keep bodies of water healthy.

Extreme Lifestyles

In some lakes, ponds, and rivers, there are places that are very salty and others that are very hot. Most organisms would die in these places, but certain microbes live there and flourish. We're going to look at these microorganisms and their extreme **habitats**.

Boiling bacteria

You probably know of Yellowstone National Park, Wyoming. There, boiling water bubbles out of the ground from **hot springs** that form pools, mud pots, and geysers (spouts of water). *Therm* means heat, and **thermophilic** microbes are those that flourish in hot places.

Thermophilic algae, bacteria, and archaea love hot springs like this one in Yellowstone National Park, Wyoming. The colors around the edges of the pool are created by thermophilic microbes.

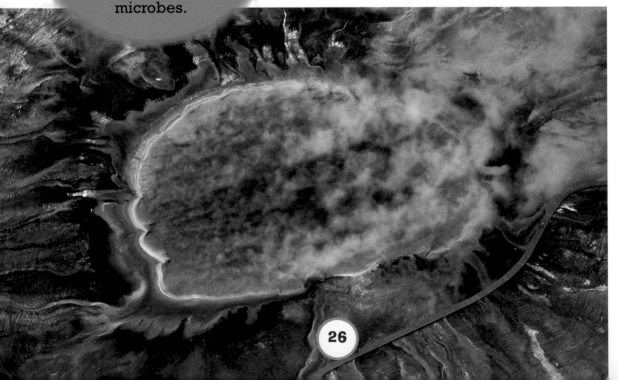

Only halophilic organisms can live in the salty waters of Salt Lake, Utah.

Salty survivors

The Dead Sea between Jordan and Israel got its name because nothing can live in its super-salty waters. Well . . . almost nothing!

Halophilic bacteria, algae, and archaea are microbes that exist in salty waters. Salt Lake in Utah and Owens Lake in California are other large, salty bodies of water where halophiles live.

Archaea

As we saw earlier, archaea have a whole domain to themselves. But there is a lot we don't yet know about this group of organisms. Until recently, archaea were only detected in extreme places, such as hot springs and salt lakes. The archaea below live in salty water, but now scientists are learning that archaea exist in many other places, too. Like bacteria, they have simple, prokaryotic cells. Archaea are very tiny, ranging from 1 to 15 micrometers in size.

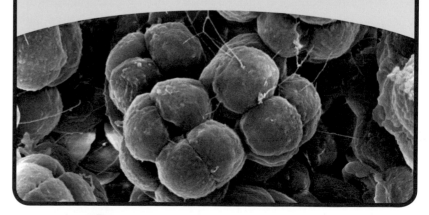

Size and Scale

In this book, we measure some things in millimeters and even smaller measurements. This is because inches are just too big for measuring microorganisms and microscopic parts of things. Millimeters are pretty small, and micrometers and **nanometers** are so tiny that they are impossible to see with the naked eye and hard to imagine. There are more than 25 million nanometers in just one inch!

1 inch =	**25.4 millimeters**
1 millimeter =	**1,000 micrometers or 1,000,000 nanometers**
1 micrometer =	**1,000 nanometers**

Only the smallest of microorganisms are measured in nanometers. Some of these, such as the tiniest bacteria and archaea, have to be magnified thousands of times before we can see them. Other microorganisms are huge compared to bacteria and archaea, but we still need to magnify them to see them clearly.

About Microscopes

Many of the images you have looked at were produced using an electron microscope. Electron microscopes can magnify things hundreds of thousands of times, so they are used to magnify archaea, bacteria, and tiny parts of cells.

At home or in school, we use optical microscopes. They usually magnify things anywhere between 20 and 1,000 times, depending on the lenses used. It's always fun to take an everyday object, like a leaf from the yard or a drop of water, and look at it under the microscope. Some of the images we have seen were made by optical microscopes with cameras attached.

Grow Your Own Microorganisms

Raising protists

If you would like to see some protists under a microscope, it's possible to raise them yourself. First you need an adult to help you make hay culture. You do this by putting a handful of dry grass in a pan of water. Bring the mixture to the boil and boil it for at least 15 minutes. Put the water in a bowl. After about a week, you will see a layer of scum containing bacteria forming on the water's surface. Then add some water from a nearby river, lake, or pond. It will contain protists that will reproduce in your water.

Growing *Spirogyra*

The alga *Spirogyra* is common in many bodies of water. If you find *Spirogyra*, put a few strands in a plastic bag and collect some of the water in a jar. When you get home, tear a *Spirogyra* strand into small pieces. You can use a pin to do this. Put the pieces in the jar of pond water and leave the jar in a sunny place. As the cells divide, your pieces of *Spirogyra* will grow into long strands again!

Glossary

algae—protists that are similar to plants

archaea—organisms with only one cell and similar to bacteria

bacteria—microorganisms with only one cell that are the smallest and most numerous life-forms on Earth

biofilm—film made of bacteria and other microbes that forms on surfaces in damp places

cell—tiny unit that all livings things are made of

cyanobacteria—type of water-dwelling bacteria that live in strands or clumps and resemble plants and algae

domains—major groups that all living things on Earth belong to: eukaryota, bacteria, and archaea. Animals, plants, and fungi are all eukaryota.

eukaryotic—describing cells or organisms, such as plants, animals, or protists, that have cells with a nucleus and other complex parts

fertilize—start the process of reproduction

fungi—organisms similar to plants but with no ability to make food, so they live on other organisms (living or dead)

habitat—place that is home to a particular plant, animal, or other organism

halophilic—salt-loving

hot spring—place where water heated deep in the ground comes up to the surface

larva—stage of an insect after it has hatched from an egg but is not yet an adult

microanimal—tiny bug or other animal too small to be seen clearly without a microscope

microbe—microorganism that is not a microanimal, such as bacteria or archaea

micrometer—measurement of length that is one-thousandth of a millimeter

microorganism—any living thing that is too small to be seen properly without a microscope

nanometer—measurement of length that is one-millionth of a millimeter

nucleus—part of a cell that controls the cell's form and functions

nutrient—substance that is a building block for living things and helps them grow and stay healthy

organism—any living thing, such as a plant, animal, or bacterium

photosynthesis—process by which plants and algae use sunlight to combine carbon dioxide and water and make food

prey—living thing hunted or caught by another for food

prokaryotic—describing cells or organisms, such as bacteria and archaea, that have a simple cell structure

protist—usually single-celled microorganism that lives in water or damp places. Protists can be plant-like (algae) or animal-like (protozoa).

protozoa—protists that are similar to animals

tentacle—long, flexible, arm-like part of an animal, such as those on an octopus, used for feeling and grasping objects

thermophilic—heat-loving

Explore These Web Sites

Wim van Egmond/Stereo/Photo/Micro
http://home.tiscali.nl/~t936927/home.html
Wander though a wonderful Web site about watery microlife. Look at the Freshwater Collection in the Micropolitan Museum!

HowStuff Works: How Extremophiles Work
http://science.howstuffworks.com/cellular-microscopic-biology/extremophile.htm
Learn more about extremophiles and where they live.

Index